*For Michael and
Teda — Blessings to
you both
Dennis*

Leaves from the World Tree

Selected Poems of
Craig Deininger
and Dennis Patrick Slattery

Cover Design by Jennifer Leigh Selig

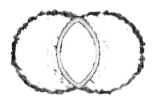

MANDORLA BOOKS
SACRAMENTO, CA
WWW.MANDORLABOOKS.COM

To read poetry is to grasp an imagined form in the making.

~Louise Cowan

TABLE OF CONTENTS

CRAIG DEININGER

DENNIS PATRICK SLATTERY

INTRODUCTION

This volume is a testament to the imagination, and to the possibilities which can be made to exist through fortunate word-arrangements when they are generous enough to come. After a decade-long engagement with mythology and depth psychology (and a lifelong engagement with poetry), I have come to recognize that imagination is among the most significant and misunderstood features in the human experience. Henry Corbin, a scholar of mystic Sufism and a colleague of Carl Jung, presents imagination as both an internal psychic organ and as an autonomous dimension in which intelligible and material planes interact. By this reckoning, the imagination is an interface where matter is spiritized and where spirit is given body in the form of image. Corbin fittingly calls this dimension the *Mundus Imaginalis*.

The substance that constitutes the *Mundus Imaginalis* is highly immaterial, yet not entirely. For the physicality of the images which take form within it can be affirmed easily enough as synaptic firings through neural networks or through thought waves in the mind, just as a gust of wind outside my window, although invisible, is affirmed by the swaying trees. More to the point, however, is that the phenomena we experience in the imagination do not require empirical validation, for the reality of its contents is irrefutable regardless of proof. Imagination is therefore a highly intimate and gnostic event.

To provide some sense of this nearly indescribable medium, consider sculpture and dance—two art-forms that work with distinctly different materials. The images in sculpture possess a high degree of tangibility and duration; whereas with dance, images run their course through time and space so fleetingly that they dissolve nearly as soon as they emerge. Therefore, the ethereal and evanescent quality of the images created by dance is, by analogy, a nearer representation of the nature of the substance of imaginal images. By no means is this to suggest that dance is a subtler or more imaginative art-form than sculpture is, but rather to attempt an approach toward the description of the matter of the imaginal image *per se*.

The important aspect here is entering into (and sustaining presence within) this environment—a task which is, fortunately, easier done than said. For example, one need only to close the eyes and imagine Williams's red wheelbarrow glazed with rainwater—and sure, throw in some white chickens. And there it is, the indisputable image, with no need to complicate the method of getting there. Besides, to provide instructions on how to imagine is a lot like providing instructions on how to laugh, cry, or yawn. We just do it; and, like anything, the more we practice and familiarize ourselves with this terrain, the more capable our image-making becomes.

In the case of poetry, we can attend to the substance and texture of the sounds themselves, which are also images of an auditory sort. Dylan Thomas's *Poetic Manifesto* is perhaps the best example of expository writing on this, and certainly the most sensual. Even when read silently, the features of voice, rhythm, and tone resound in the inner ear, and are real. The case is the same for the images that poetry sculpts, dances, and paints through narrative. They are perceived by the inner eye and, also, are real. Further, we can go on to say that even the meanings and ideas possess a materiality, albeit of an even more profound subtlety which I am quite incapable of approaching in expository terms. The unanswerable question is where does matter end and pure spirit begin? Well, I suppose poetry, and indeed all art-forms, attempt an answer by getting as close as possible to this point without passing over into pure transcendence.

For my part, these poems represent a significant portion of a lifetime, composed between the ages of 20 and 50. With hundreds to choose from, this selection comprises what I judge to be the best sixty-ish pages I could compile. Due to this span, inconsistencies in content and voice are unavoidable. Depending on what age or phase of life in which they were composed, some of the poems are settled and thoughtful while others are reckless and risky. I have decided to include these latter, written in signature *puer aeternus* style, for the simple reason that they are accurate representatives of a natural phase of a human life.

James Hillman approaches the *puer aeternus* as a figure replete with impatience, irresponsibility, and misdirection, yet also as a wellspring of creative energy. The counterbalance to this figure is the *senex*, the seasoned, experienced, and wise figure. Conversely, the positive attributes of the *puer aeternus* are enthusiasm, versatility, and a seemingly unending store of energy. And the negative aspects of the *senex* are disenchantment, stubbornness, and fatigue. These energies, or archetypes, are best represented in Greek mythology as Hermes and Chronos, respectively, and they are present within all of us. They delineate the two poles of the puer-senex dyad. Just as the practice of sustaining a balance between the tangible and intelligible aspects of the *Mundus Imaginalis* is conducive to the creation and apperception of images, so the balancing of the puer and senex energies is a highly potent path to the creation of quality art. It has been my endeavor to lift the positive aspects of each while carrying the negative aspects which necessarily accompany, and sometimes, bolster them.

Dennis and I have been building this book over the past two years. I believe that our mutual passion for mythology, imagination, symbolism, and depth psychology provides a unique and unifying undercurrent to the contents herein. I'd like to add that Dennis was among my most inspiring professors during my mythology studies at Pacifica Graduate Institute, where we delved into mythic material, pursuing possibilities of meaning or interpretation or whatever other phenomena with great passion—nor did we forego the experiential aspects of the literature. Our most memorable class occurred at sea. We had just completed a thorough engagement with the epic poem *Moby Dick* (and to those who believe the tale to be a work of prose, allow me to gently rebuke: Read slower). Regardless, on that day we attended to the experience first-hand as we put out to sea. A pod of dolphins raced and wove in the bow-wake, periodically launching high in the air, apparently showing off—or better, just inclined to be joyful because why not. Although we did not encounter the White Whale, we did encounter many other nautical aspects of the poem along with a blue whale. To this day, I still recall the distinct scent of the whale's balmy breath as it passed over the deck like steam. Perhaps we did not experience the magnitude of transformation that Jonah did when he was swallowed whole, but the majority of the class felt that getting misted by this ancient wonder was sufficient.

Fortunately, with literary narrative and imagery, one can attain a good many experiential boons, and without literally jumping into an ocean—which I once accomplished in Alaska in my younger days and nearly drowned in a pod of beluga whales. Thirty years hence, however, I'd rather just read about it. Similarly, with these poems by Dennis and myself, we invite you to sample some of these experiences in the wild and limitless interior of the imagination.

Craig Deininger

SELECTED POEMS OF
CRAIG DEININGER

for Leah

I Nondescript Vicissitudes

Obdurate Enlightenments

Answers, I release you
from your questions.

Questions, good luck.
Beginnings, I love you, strolling

through the wreckage, toe-ing the debris.
Matter, you can let go of Maya anytime.

A rain of shooting stars.

The fall is beautiful when it's all
or nothing all at once. So many lines

of liquid light score the dark

and fade. Ego, I suggest
you surrender to the miracles

that make the miraculous possible.
Or, you can have terms of surrender

imposed upon you less miraculously.

Sacred scripture declares surrender
wins the kingdom every time

though some might disagree. Vikings,
for example.

Republicans, too.

When my car broke down
my friend said a space for something new

had been carved into my misfortune.
It's new not having a car, if that's what he means.

When it comes to loss I'm more
like a Republican Viking than a mystic savant.

I just resist the terms.

But maybe I'll come around
and give this mystic business

a go. I could grab my Viking-axe
and set to chopping tons of wood.

I could carry all this water.

Event

At sixteen, unannounced and unprepared for, the huge
alien spacecraft descended upon me in the twilit hours.

It closed out the entire sky and waited.

And I did precisely what any sixteen-year-old should.
With arms upraised and outstretched, I offered

myself up to be their guest, their passenger.
Indiana, at the time, seemed small and I had questions.

Several ages, or perhaps seconds, ticked by
as the variables were weighed.

But no rampway was sent down.

Nor was I beamed up. Instead, they rose
slowly into the sky, paused

a moment, and shot off
at what I could only guess to be the speed of light.

They never came back.

Still, I remained for some time
looking off into the long empty corridor of space

that had hosted their trajectory.
I had questions.

Chasing the Elusive Fall-Poem

The fall comes early this year
and the hawk-eyed poets turn

once more to the crisping

sun, to read the signs
as they drift the sky's dry pool.

Dusk deepens
as we take up the pen. The forest

puts on a glow and sighs.
One by one

she drops her fires to the floor.
An anxious doe tiptoes across the page

and the last honeybee races home like a gold bullet.

Porchlights dust the countryside
while our desperate words,

our brittle lives, flicker like moths
and catch in the wattage.

Yet who's to say
we're not thence kindled and blown

through fields of powdered stars?

And are these not ample tidings
to walk wayward into the fire?

A good fall-poem drives

a hard bargain, no getting around that.

But the days are fading fast
and rumors of sleep sweep the land.

Something stirs

in its den as another year beds down.
Huge and awake in its wreath of fur, something

steps into the atmosphere, noses the wind
and begins.

Fergus

I love my cat.
I love the way he holds vigil

at the window, a witness to the world
of trees and grass, soft chewy birds.

I love my cat, fanned in the blast
of invisible suns, the smelted copper

and godlight coming off.

I love the spaciousness of unguessable thoughts
roaming over and under

the warm hill between his ears.
I love the subtle tufts that his ears end in

and the thinness of the ears themselves
which flicker like candles in a drafty room

or by my lightly touching them.

I love his insane fluffiness, goddammit!
I love when he cleans it in long rhythmic laps

of the tongue, and when he suddenly stops
to look up

as if he'd just remembered

something very important—or at me,
as if something very important were happening

and that I was clearly missing it.

I love his industrious crunching
when he sets to over his food bowl,

and his vacant gaze when he pees in his box.

I love the meticulousness
with which he rakes the litter

over his work, the maestro forepaw
feathering the grade.

I love when he leaps like water
from the floor to the bed and pushes out

a single mew. And the purring that follows,
the seamless thunder of a distant stormfront

coming my way.

I love the stalwart engine
whence all his thunder comes,

the stout little plum
between those paw-sized lungs

under all that fur.

I Would Travel Thusly

If I could diffuse
above a black lake at dawn and roll

in the licking mist while some kilted fellow
piped songs from the dock. And if I could ride

the notes through the trees and run bare

with deer down vapor trails and think
nothing of the cold damp earth,

of the slick jet stones
beneath my milky feet.

Aye, then would I travel thusly.

And if I could sing a single note
as clear and as pitched

as the sun that sprays flame
through a waterlogged sky,

then my soul would sound
from the edge of this world.

Alas, if I could bend my final door
from the mist and the light,

then would I spring, gather
my chances

and promptly step through.

How the Godhead Was Delved and Builded

beats me. But, and more importantly,
I'd like to have forearms like God's

as rendered by Michelangelo in the Sistine,
minus the antiquity, the chips

of plaster pulling away.

That way I could look down on them
any time and be pleased.

At any rate, work goes quickly
in this trade, dealing with dimensions

and thresholds. The term *king-stud*, I think,

deserves mention and is a favorite
among builders and non-builders alike.

But I prefer the finish-work
when jambs are set with brass striker-plates

and doors are mortised to receive their hinges
which, if well-placed, can be cunningly made

to swing out upon kickass vistas.

I suppose the forearm is a working part
of the deal, too—a hammer of sorts

torqueing the fist that torques the helve
that pins the head. I like that word—*torque*.

Thus do we sink whatever into soft pine two-bys.

And this is good because the truth is
we don't know how the godhead was delved

and builded. We don't!

But at least we've got jobs. And awesome forearms.
And kickass vistas to be swung into.

Grace

I looked up at the sky, some stars, some cloudwrack
illumined in moonlight.

And although it was not particularly spectacular, it was
what I was looking at.

I've watched plenty of stars sail through moonlit cloudwrack.
Sometimes it's on, sometimes not.

It all depends on whatever.

The point is more like this, please bear with me,
it was stars and cloudwrack, outline of trees. Leafless,

nothing special
during my moment of what is.

Another night somewhere in a soul.

I looked up at nothing that was there and said thank you
because it was very beautiful, an encounter

I had earlier that day

that had nothing to do with anything
except that I was there.

Desert Poem

The desert is a beast of flame. With a heart
of flame. It watches and it waits.

It has precisely all the time in the world.
Lizards zip across the rocks like tongues
of flame. Their shadows are flaming

shadows. The desert is an unending devourer
that devours itself without end.

In the spring it fans itself into flowers.

Their beauty is like a moment of roaring flame.
In or out of the desert, wherever one goes,

there is only the desert.

Still, wrapped in flame,
flame-furred, the mirage of the non-desert resides.

Night builds and rises like a tide.

Elsewhere and otherworldly, jellyfish
propel themselves

through vats of moonlight, a liquid cougar
clears the rim and dissolves, a poet

takes a stab at a poem, shoulders his pack
and steps out into a blizzard of stars.

The Quick Lizard Passages

i

In the dry desert heat there is no relief,
but to those who will hear, the quick lizard
shuttles over the rocks
and thrums the rumor of rain.

ii

Those who have traveled by night
through the quick lizard's realm
agree the constellations are poorly construed.
For nearly every species of lizard
can be plotted therein.

iii

When the moon is waxed
full in the east and the sun burns
low in the west, the quick lizard aims south
with an eye on each and has the two
contend in his mind.

iv

Fortunate is he who has seen,
through the bright black night, the Pleiades
fixed in the grease
of the quick lizard's eye.

v

After nightfall, when the desert melts into shadow
and the distant city is a smudge of light,
the quick lizard sits on his rock
and takes pause to consider the smudge.

vi

When the meteors streak down and rend the nightsky
like wands of whitefire one after the next,
the quick lizard arranges himself just-so
and makes them his backdrop.

vii

To those with patience
and incalculable stealth, at dawn
can be seen the just-risen sun
fully eclipsed by the quick lizard's head.

viii

In the desert there is only one path
which the quick lizard knowingly walks without end.
Thus do the wise consider the lizard
before walking the path.

ix

The quick lizard faces always to wind,
for he is most sleek and the passing is a pleasure
to them both. At times, however, he turns
this way or that, to stir things up
and chisel his features.

x

When the full blown moon wheels up
into the sky and pours her metal over the land,
then is the quick lizard most at ease.
He slips into his mercury robe
and selects a form to suit his design.

Solve et Coagula

Portal Rim, Moab

It's getting on into July
and the blast-furnace is stoked.

Once again I make my stand, far from town,

jacked up into the flame on a slab of rock.
The rubble and slag-heaps stretch out

before me. Towers of solid rock groan and waver
in the distance. And the merciless sun

strides through the wreckage, clanging
his cymbals and trilling the air.

Despite these, I press on to some end.

As molten stock I walk the anvil-face
and stagger between blows, breathing fire

myself, a great iron lung hinged on two legs,
bending this way and that. I breathe and stagger,

and breathe again. And so it goes
until the fire wheels over the rim of the world

and leaves me here in the growing night
to harden beneath the stars.

II *Alchemical Engagements*

Hoffmann's Angel

descended.

So I opened
myself to the moment

which smote my tongue
like a condensed star, an infinitesimal electric grain.

In yonder gallery we've got fractals!
and Alex Grey painting an Alex Grey

painting an Alex Grey painting called
Seraphic Transport Docking on the Third Eye.

As one might expect, it depicts a seraphic transport
docking on a third eye

which is pretty much what happened next.

Along with some other things
to which my words exert beautifully

hopeless efforts to touch but then

when dealing in ineffables
the question is not whether words will fail

but rather how they will fail
and what brief reports

might somehow clear a path
or ride a miracle back from ground zero

to the embodied soul.

Like this deity
who has just emerged in the south

end of the living room near the bookcase.

I don't know the term for effortlessly brushing
quantum foam aside like drifts of snow,

but that's what she's doing.
Beside her on the desk, towering

in atmosphere above the long undulating slab
of polished wood, a pile of microdots.

Tiny purple barrels strewn like neon
boulders in a park. Someone's modern art project

way down there.

I'm thinking about eating them all
and then seeing what happens but ten is a lot.

One is a lot. I'll hold off and maintain eternal presence
with awesome interdimensional entities for a while.

And then write poems for them when eternity
inevitably smears into tomorrow

and all the rapturous players, done
with flying, done with pouring

libations over the stunned neophyte,

fold their tired wings, load up
and roll out of town.

Muse

For a while there she was running with me
hand in hand and then she let me fall

on my face and I love her.

And now I get to consider all the reasons
why, being so many versions of beautiful.

Beyond the beauty there is simply she
and less simply I

with an upraised hand
awkwardly waving goodbye

and hello. Some of the terrains
I enter are fragile. And precious

in consciousness.

Breathe on them and they shatter.
Breathe on them and they burgeon.

I have found the lonely frontier.
Or close enough. Sometimes I think

it's the distance that makes the revelation possible.

In which case I wonder what fewer revelations
might be like. I was thinking

about maybe coming home for a while.
Not yet she says.

The Last Ship

It was the end of the world and everybody
was anxious.

We had been dreaming about this for years.

The world-tree rose from the flood
like a tower, its leaves lost to winter.

We were making good time, thronging
the deck

when a man pointed back through the distance
to the receding world-tree now vague in mist.

He'd seen muses at play, swimming

and frolicking like dolphins about the bole.
We got excited and begged the captain to pull around

for the muses, but Captain held his course
and chewed his cigar.

We pleaded like children, including
the children. *Christ!* he rumbled

and swung us round. We cheered. Everyone
was happy. Even Captain smiled somewhat.

One pass! he stammered and sounded
the horn. A hushed silence fell over all

as the world-tree drew near. We strained
through the mist and therein did perceive

forms, bobbing up and down and around the bole.

But then we saw it was just dolphin-colored debris
from the end of the world moved by the water

in the likeness of play.

Captain turned us hard-about
and set us back on course. It was no surprise, it was

as if it never happened.

We bore ourselves well for the end of the world,
the rigging of our jaws, our chins

thrust like prows into the weather, we sailed on
and didn't look back. And the cold

dolphin-colored mist wrapped itself around the ship
and made our faces sleek to look upon.

The Slopper

* an alchemical term referencing those practitioners whose exclusive
endeavor was the production of elemental gold

The slopper reveled in heaps
of gold. They cascaded beautifully down

like steep banks
of sand and debris collapsing upon themselves.

He had succeeded in his little laboratory experiment,
transmuting base-metals into gold

which he had heaped
because heaps were far more thrilling, more awesome,

than meticulously organized stacks.
One heap in particular,

he had heaped most magnificently,
admixing gold dust and gold leaf

topped with slabs
that slid like ice floes hewn from solid gold.

The place was a gold mess.

While lounging in all his gold, the slopper slept
and dreamed of nothing

but gold. In his dream it swallowed him whole
and everything went black.

He was in the cold dark heart of gold.
There was an element

of resistance somewhere in the deeps
of himself. It was a terrible dream.

So he woke and decided
not to worry about it. Every night

he slept in his gold and every night he dreamed
dark dreams

until one morning he woke and found
he'd been swallowed

up to his neck in gold.
It was not a dream. He could not get out.

He struggled and cried for help.
His grief echoed for days through chambers of gold.

There was nowhere to go so he slept once more.
But this time he dreamed

his spiritual friend pulled him out, saying, 'Behold,
I have found treasure

in a worthless heap of gold. My dear friend whom I love lives.
I have lifted him from the cold dark heart of gold.'

The slopper woke and waited a long time
for his spiritual friend to arrive. But then he remembered

he had no spiritual friends.
He would have to dig himself out and find one.

Or dig one out of himself.

The Poet-Carpenter Reflects on Weather During His Morning Break

Winter, Sonoma County

The wind, intent
on blasting the slopes and trees with sidelong rain

for weeks on end has outdone itself

and opened a door to the land of the living,
a thin brief piece of blue barely held

in shreds of cloud. So I reach

my naked hand up from the damp
Ovidian underworld halls and am surprised

it doesn't catch and burn away. Nay,
the hand survives

with the rest of the body now washed
in precious light, and a fey mood

compels me to rally and announce

that I am not a vampire! Behold
I do not kindle in sun, am not become

a heap of ash! Surround me with mirrors
and reflect shall I.

Sop that bread in garlic sauce
and hand it over. Pierce my heart

with wooden stakes and

actually don't pierce my heart with wooden stakes.

But no one hears because no one is here.
Save the ravens, those vague black shrouds

perched in mist

and the salamander hoards
pushing through the loam like extinguished brands.

And the moment is passed, the window

closed over again. Everywhere rivers
of mist roll by, now rising

now sinking as the contours prescribe.
Across the widest one

I half-believe I see
the slow gray shades of Orpheus

and Eurydice.

But it's just the neighbor and his wife
walking the road.

'I thought you were mythic figures
come to keep me company in the underworld,' I say.

'Nope,' says Joe, 'We're up here in California.
Come on by for lunch if you can find a way.'

'Is it far?' I ask.

'It is,' he answers, 'But not in miles.'
And suddenly they are gone. And the rain resumes.

'Not in miles,' I muse and drift

to the shed, load ten bags of concrete
onto the quad and drive it down

to the pour.

Renewal

I love the way small birds light
on twigs half their weight

and step into their godhood.

So quietly pending
on the limb of a limb ad infinitum.

Today it happened in full sunlight, smeared
on the leaves like wax.

The shudder, the subsequent
bounce and then

this present bird,

this exquisite engine
idling in the center of everything.

And I realized that poise is burden
borne well, and that a bird on a limb

coined equilibrium, a rift

through which God pours
in a torrent of water and feathers.

But then I turned to something important
or pressing

though I no longer remember what or why.

And the world dimmed.
And fifty-thousand angels, more or less,

receded into their robes.

Here a leaf, there a stone.
'I see you,' I said as I walked away.

And now that whatever pressing thing
it was that I forgot has burgeoned

into an urgency, I'm just going to breathe
and write a poem about this bird

in case all those angels come back.
In case poetry can make that happen.

Approaching the Goddess

But let my cry stretch out behind me
Like a road on which I have followed you.
And sustain me for my time in the desert
On what is essential to me.
~W. S. Merwin, *"Lemuel's Blessing"*

In the wild
interior

everything's worn
down to essence.

The howling wind, the long tracts
of empty space

and I

who have forgotten food
and learned to drink water off the wind,

off the shade of a stone.

In search of you I have carved
through desert fire,

slept in frost
on canyon floors

stretched beneath their rivers of stars.

At times I hear them, the voices
of my pack

echo in the past. They are gone.
Lost.

I am the last.

My mat of fur holds more seasons
than I can remember, more journeys

than I can count.
It is the ravaged banner of a life

draped over a frame
and my proudest achievement.

Lean, alert, drawn

toward and blown back by the goal,
the practice here is precarious.

A careful admixture of caution and chance,
to slice thin slices of approach.

To barely proceed but proceed
into the storm

of beauty as she bends into life.

Massive desire drives me on,
reverence keeps me at bay.

The conflict I bear, the engine
in a heart that none can see. It glows

like a myth
wrought in ancient fire by some forgotten god.

It is hers.

I've wrapped it in a beast
because nothing else can carry it.

Excavation

Inner work has little to do
with psychology. It's more

like archeology. And one
quickly finds how deep

the rabbit-hole
goes.

Some go in
with tractors and chains

to raise the rapture of heaven
and hell locked at the throats.

Survivors convert to brushes
and breath.

Sometimes speaking, sometimes
silent, but always a gentle breath

to stir the centuries and wake the dust
of ancient souls.

Our ancient souls.

Refusal of the Call

The other day there came a fog.
So I walked to its edge

and spoke into it just to see what would happen.
I asked, of course, if there are answers in the fog.

And the fog quite startled me when it replied

and said I'd have to enter and find out for myself.
So I asked if I entered would I ever want to leave.

And the fog said no, I would never want to leave.
So I asked if Truth is the element

that would keep me from ever wanting to leave.

And the fog said I'd have to enter and find out for myself.
So I said no, that it all sounded pretty sketchy to me.

And the fog said fine.

Goddess

There is nothing to do a goddess told me.
She was up in a tree in bloom,

cascades when the wind slid through.

Simply to be she called through petals and snow
is a total and supreme act.

'Can I come on up there and kiss you?' I asked.

She smiled and departed on roads of glass.
'I get it,' I called, 'Simply to be!'

But she was gone. Really gone. So I carried her absence
home and built a wonderful religion

around it, replete with intricate rites
and precipitous passages to keep me honed

in the event of her return.

Come back is its theme and *You're beautiful* is mostly
what it says. I know, she told me simply to be.

But I'm not in it simply to be.
I'm going for the kiss.

Passage North

I shall hang in the taiga-lush with the members
of the trees and learn to speak in long and windy languages.

I shall rinse my thoughts with water
and stack them in the snow.

And then I will go.

I will not stop until the compass needle cracks.
I shall attain the icefields,

and when I grow weary of white
I will shake the sun into flakes.

I shall sink my love into the fathoms
of dog-fur.

I shall ride the icebergs through the soup
and clap the surface squarely with my feet.

I shall slip into the salt and glide whale-silent
through fields of cobalt under the ice.

I shall plant myself upon magnetic north
and crackle in the charge.

I shall recline in the veil of the northern lights
and shape them into dragons.

They will sprinkle me with lime and confer
among themselves:

What shall we do with this one?

III   Epiphanies of the Rad

Stellar Explosions

When the mushrooms kicked in, my girlfriend's face
exploded into owls. And my cat who now was pinging
off the walls—well, there were owls in the house.
One, its face flat as an anvil, exploded
the plate-glass window and sailed off
into the night such that it remained
eerily backlit by the mystery of the moon.
'Wow,' I said, and went back to my faceless girlfriend
to tell her of the awesome symbol I had beheld
through exploded glass. She said I used that word
too much. It was strange hearing words
emerge from a mouthless face
that wasn't there. So I entered the Hall of Knowledge
which was formerly the hall to the bathroom
and conferred with some misshapen owls who objected
their feathers were merely ruffled. They said it was okay
to be excessive like that, assuring me explosions
were exceptionally ambitious expansions
even though they preferred gliding silences.
I was so happy I told them I loved them.
I exploded *I love you!* to the owls.
They blinked and said nothing.
'Look,' said one, 'I'm a lighthouse
revolving my lamps over the churning nightsea
bestrewn with dark reefs and other nameless perils.'
My cat sprinted over the dark reefs and then sprinted
back again, something I never thought I'd see in this lifetime.
The other nameless perils took shape beyond the reefs
and for some reason looked really good.
But the home environment was getting out
of hand. I was compelled to regroup. First, I folded
my dirty laundry and stacked it neatly back in the hamper.
Then I returned to the realm of exploded glass
and summoned the owls thither

with my electric cello, bowing the sacred chords.
And behold, they came, fleet and swift
like a keening freight train of iron and feathers
that rushed out in almost perfect silence.
When the last owl had flown and their distant train
spiraled like a thread into the watery deeps of the moon,
I returned to my girlfriend to see how she was doing.
But she had exploded into a new reality
of diaphanous textures and rippling hues.
I carefully addressed the fabric of her being
and told it its beautiful face was en route for the moon.
'I just thought you should know that,' I said
and collapsed like a star into the big black
fluffy chair.

All Ye Dysfunctional Poets, Rock On

Whosoever increaseth in wisdom
increaseth also in sorrow.
This is the formula handed us
by Solomon the Wise. And poetry that lacks
in wisdom sucks. So we set out
with our busted marriages and compounding loans
into the field of sorrows to increase our poetry
at breakneck speeds. We scamper
like squirrels across the lanes, getting nicked
and dinged as we go. And that is why
so many of us have mangled tails.
Or even no tails.
We press on, making all the wrong choices
for all the right reasons. There is madness
to our method. And I don't mean that subtle
ironic Shakespearean madness, either.
I mean the other kind.
Tired and decrepit, staggering through the streets
in our wayworn threadbare tweeds,
we are professionals. And we have a knack
for getting the art clobbered out of us.
Time and again, we rush the tower of beauty
with its vision of promise and hope and break
to pieces upon it. But we stand ourselves
in the end, brush the dust from our jackets
and shuffle home in the wake of another day
shot down. And all that remains is the wild
wreckage of our desperate lives.
And the magnificent poems.

Allow Me to Clarify

When I said your girlfriend has beautiful eyes
I did not mean I wished to gaze, to plunge,
into them like a tumult of chariots rushing
to the din of horses down the strand with oceans
rising and falling, pitching in balmy darkness
of vaulted interiors where stacked tiers
of archangels sing in tremulous unison
Glo-o-o-o-o-o-ria with such blast of resonance
that the earth, a moment, trembles, loses her breath,
and then catches it again as if for the first time.
I just meant she has beautiful eyes.

Bad Drugs

I suppose I should write it, of all things,
the PCP poem to inspire the youth. It was 1985
and apparently someone thought it'd be fun
to lace their ditchweed and sell it to some kids.
Blazing down the interstate we knew right away
we were way too high. I suspected it was PCP
because our biology teacher had told us
about two best friends who smoked some
in New Hampshire, and the one threw the other
off a mountain. But we were in Indiana
and not worried about mountains.
A decade later I met a dude in my poetry
program, the only other adult I know
who has had the experience and he
said it best, 'Dude, we knew right away
we were way too high,' which is why
I worded it that way earlier. Not only were we
way too high, we were way too fucked.
Complicated psychic structures emerged
from some adjacent apocalypse
and took their places on the road, forcing
us to scream and swerve. A lot.
We landed in a strange, disjuncted, wobbly basement
where atmospheres advanced and receded
like tides. Everything was different and funny. We laughed
at how different and funny everything was until Bowers
transformed into a *wer*-thing from *The Howling*
and morphed some big-ass fangs.
So I busted out my chucks and swiveled on over there
like five helicopters chained together through space
to destroy him. I was also told that I knocked myself out.
Probably during the precarious neck-wrap.
It had happened before in practice.
Some thirty years later I am compelled

to counsel the uninitiated to remain so
on this one. But if you're determined
and totally stupid, then have it. And bring
the chucks. They just might save you.

The Rapid Bat Passages

i

The rapid bat is an amalgam of oiled blades,
keen and bright, for how else does he so unctuously
scissor the night?

ii

The world of the rapid bat comprises
countless doors opening and closing like an applause.
He cuts accordingly, edgewise or flat,
and shoots them all with echoes.

iii

Batlets, being young bats, are like bruised thumbs.
For they are singular digits
suppressed unto mute.

iv

The rapid bat is much like a greased hinge
sundered from its jamb and thence cannoned
insanely into the night.

v

The rabid bat is exceptionally rapid
for a madness fills him to pierce
and inflict.

vi

Many bats packed shoulder to shoulder
are wondrously insulative and could be called,
in certain circles, batting.

vii

The bat and the satchel are brethren
if one thinks long enough on it, for each holds
a darkness and a stressed front a.

viii

The wise should do well
to sympathize with the plight of the bat,
for he is naught but an unfortunate mouse
propelled through the darkness on wings.

ix

The rigid vessel of the rational mind
pitched itself against the vault of night
and shattered thence
into a euphony of bats.

x

It is no coincidence that the word 'acrobatics'
is sometimes used among English-speaking peoples.

xi

Finer cathedrals surely would be
were one to cypher the script of the bat
and translate from ether to stone.

—

A Brief Exchange at Gate B7

'Are you a wisdom-keeper?' she asked,
looking up from the times.
'No,' he said, 'I am a sorrow-bearer.'
'Oh,' she said, 'That sounds heavy.'
'It is,' he said, shaking his head, 'It is. But
the weight of sorrow is light
when you know what and why you bear.'
'That's pretty deep,' she said, 'Okay,
I'll go out with you.'
'That's great news,' he said, 'Even if it goes badly.'
'Oh, you've been injured?'
'My left knee, yes.'
He pointed to the knee.
'I meant emotionally,' she said.
'I know,' he conceded.
Then she scanned him
with her electronic device.
'There is conflict in you, sorrow-bearer,' she said
and went back to the times.
A dark expanse had settled between them, he thought,
beyond repair, just long tracts of lonely space.
'So, I'll pick you up at seven in Detroit?' he ventured.
'I'm sorry,' she said, 'But I'm really not interested.'
'Thank you,' he said, 'The pain of your departure
has deepened me.'

Thus Did We Get Real Good at Grammar and Sundry

'I love the way you omitted the comma after *Love*
when you signed *Love Jeffrey*,' she said.
'How come?' I asked, closing my book.
'Because,' she said, 'it smacks of the imperative.
And I love it when you tell me what to do . . . sometimes.'
'Smacking of the imperative could be reworded
the imperative's smack,' I suggested,
evoking the genitive contraction.
'Awesome,' she said. 'Well done, indeed.'
'Exclamation point!' I ejected recklessly.
'No,' she said, crossing her arms,
'That doesn't work. It's too overt.'
'But I thought the phallic—'
'Please stop,' she said.
'Question mark?' I ventured.
'I like that,' she said, 'Question mark is nice.'
'Question mark,' I said confidently.
'Mmmmm,' she said.
Then I tried hyphen
and she said 'Oh yes!'
So I said it a whole bunch of times
then switched on over to parenthetical to vary it up.
'Too smart,' she said, catching her breath,
'Go back to hyphen.' So I clocked
back in on hyphen for a few more laps
before downshifting into subject.
'As a noun?' she queried.
'As a verb,' I retorted.
'Goodness!' she exclaimed. 'As a verb!'
'Reverberation!' I cried with upraised arms.
'Don't be so ambitious,' she said. 'Either stick
with what works or say nothing.'
For a brief moment we both feared
I might do something stupid like say *nothing*.

Instead, I accepted my place in the margin
(but in the spotlight, too). *A paradox*, I thought,
Silent yet voluminous like a theme.
'—theme,' I slipped.
'No more words,' she whispered
and was right, 'No more words.'
Then she pulled out in front and secured the lead.
No more words sounded good to me.
So I just fell into place, silent
and portentous, and coasted in the slipstream
like an ellipsis.

The Meteor-Herd

In deep space there coasts a meteor-herd.
It is barely perceptible, cruising through the darkness
where the flimsy beams of the nearest star
provide the shadow of an outline for our mind's eye.
They move through pure silence
like reflections over glass.
And although this may seem
peaceful and dreamy to us, they, at times,
find it rather mundane. On occasion,
and much to their relief, they sort of clip each other
and gently roll away. However, this herd,
nearly nine thousand strong, is wise
in light-years and avoids too much of this
lest they be chipped to dust.
They therefore travel in loose formation.
And thus would they go on, sailing
through the remainder of their consistent
yet uncharted lives, except that there exists
another herd, fresh from the Omegas,
and they are an unruly bunch, recently
detonated from the Motherchunk.
And being on average
twice the size of any veteran meteor, they like
to clip each other every chance they get.
They like to clip off shelves and ledges
and whatever else they can muster-up-and-umph
themselves into. They like to do this to others
and they like to have others do it to them.
They just like the way it feels—getting clipped,
and therefore travel in a tight cluster,
coalescing and shattering, trailing a lane of gravel,
sand and dust several thousand miles long.
It so happens the two are on a collision-course.
The young ones begin to quiver as they come

into range, aching for impact, to smite or be smitten,
it makes no difference, into fine debris.
Yet, at the moment of impact, both herds, somehow,
astronomically, pass through each other
entirely untouched. Without so much as a nudge
or a hip-check. Not even the brush of a wind-like current
from a near-miss. Absolute nothing.
Well, the younger herd is not all right
with this, and is left to coast on in anguish
through the limpid, ever-yielding fabric of space.
And the elder herd coasts on, too. But they seem
less unsettled by the whole thing. They sort of nod
as they coast.

It's Good to Dissolve under a Field of Stars

Because form no longer hinders.
Because infinity has a face I can't describe just now.
Because the spaciousness of oneness is awesome.
Because we are all existants existing in existence.
Because I can give up everything
and saturate the universe with my nectary essence.
Because unending sex lasts longer.
Because I'm not wearing clothes.
In case you were wondering.
Because infinite pizza is more fulfilling
than pizza that has had limitations imposed upon it!
Because perfection is irrelevant.
Because better than perfection is inescapable.
Because I get to invent new genres
that will deepen my love for stars.
Because this is not a poem, my bleating
syllables wandered off to find their meanings.
Because I can relativize on their behalf
and be their glinting shepherd in the clear celestial north.
Because I can warm my hands
by the ember of Arcturus and discuss
cutting-edge shepherding techniques
with my star-furred neighbors Leo and Ursa.
Because I can go on adventures
where spacetime gets weird.
Because I can bring luminary devices
and send the beams through cosmic events
and watch them bend like reeds.
Because I grew up near a pond
that was edged with reeds.
Because I often saw starlight
rocking in the water there.
Because early experiences
are formative to the arc of a life.

IV Sundry Stars

The Field Goal

I was thinking I'd embrace letting go
and give it a good squeeze.

Or kick it through the uprights like a star.

Obviously, like a football star who wins
everything in the final seconds of the 4th

thereby fulfilling the hourly fantasy.
But also like a star star. You know,

those far off glinting things I can't stop writing about.
Like a gem poised in the tines

of a struck tuning fork, held
through sheer resonance alone.

Which, by the way, is what gives a star
its shimmer, its tremolo of light.

Symbolic expression lets me say things like this
and be right no matter what.

'Hey! Get your head out of the stars,' my coaches
always yell.

'I'm an angel,' I tell them, 'Go to hell.'

Here's a thought: were one to construct a forest
of towering tuning forks *in resonato*,

might one amble, saint-like, on the trembling air?
For what is a tuning fork

but a sung agreement between two poles?

And what, a human being, but an agreement
to be jumping-front-snap-kicked

by kung fu masters into brilliant vibrating matter?
Maybe the soul is that football-shaped thing

that finds its way through the uprights
and makes the incandescent fans

roar in my head.

Renaissance scholars call it the *mandorla*.
Geometers, a *vesica piscis*.

Either way, it succinctly sums the deal:
carried, kicked and thrown down the field, flags

flying everywhere until we touch down triumphant
in the end-zone.

But even with all these elaborate metaphors,
and all my careful research,

my coaches still resist when I tell them
we live inside a football, drifting

through the stars.

How About Another Poem for the Stars

Our lives fly past us now and the stars
are blown through the sky like leaves.

At times, they descend into our pools
to take on the sovereign resilience of water.

And we could learn a thing or two from this.

For are we not brief brittle things
beneath their reckoning? Even to those

no longer there, extinguished ages ago.
And to the others we've never seen

whose light yet roars through the miles

to meet us. So it is we look out from the present
upon an ancient past. A hundred billion strong

in our neighborhood alone, they say.
But which are really there? And which aren't?

And which aren't there that really are?

A difficult predicament and most inconvenient
to our number-arts. Still, an approximate

hundred billion seems ample to me
and we should not have to lose sleep over a few

winking out here or there while the slender lines

they've left behind go on speeding
through the dark. For such is the stuff of these

lighted wanderers, these incandescent crumbs
strewn by the wayside by whim or design

to mark for us some final trail to steer by.

Or maybe they're just doing their own thing
whether any are here to see them or not.

I have no answers. But I will stand here
all the same, and gaze into the deeps

and make my little guesses.

Contemplating Cosmogonies at the Pool

Children, I bet, and really loud,
cannonballing
through the
stacked
planes,
bursting them
like sheets
of glass
into
a trillion
bits
of
stars.

The Bonfire

A new group of silhouettes has risen up
against the evening sky. Their thin

and distant voices string out before them

as they descend into the field. Tonight
the cigarettes burn clean

and crisp faces slip into the light, flicker
and slip out again. One suddenly stands,

it is a girl I know from school.

Now sanctified in the orange light,
she takes on a remarkable fullness.

A gust of oak leaves rushes the hill

and I realize for the first time she is lovely
from the farthest corner down. Down

by the woods, and beside them the creek
that has been silent till now, a dark truck

lights up from within and the music begins.
But by the time it reaches us,

just some thirty yards away, the wind

has knocked the edges off, it has passed
through fire and been rinsed in starlight

and the finished themes brush past us in veils.
And although the air is run through

with wind and the whirling of voices, there is
a dark and unnameable silence that keeps us all

in awe though none of us knows it at the time.

And it is not until much later, when I have snuck
in through the bedroom window,

and am about to fall asleep, that I see clearly

the half-empty beercan tilted back against the stars,
the heavy treetops thrown in the wind, the bonfire

racing beneath an Indiana sky, beneath
the face of a beautiful girl.

The Indiana Pre-Dawn Fieldsong

We five startled

    five springing deer

        (who just caught wind of you)

  now mud flinging

      field mud kickicking

our starlit shadows

    one by one over the barbed

the barb-bound

      bound over the barbed-wire fence

River

Kasilof, Alaska

Someone tore the sky
and it poured into the mountains.

Channels of it ran like paint,
stretched through the spruce

and rushed to the sea.

The salmon are making their big run
and the waters are heavy with flesh.

Their glistening backs
break from bank to bank,

churning the tumult like fires
in ice. But soon the river

will be empty again.
They will have dispersed to the streams.

And to the smaller than streams streams.

Sixty-pound kings, now feverishly orange,
are dying in the shallows. They glide

into the gentle ebbs and begin to fall asleep.
One slowly capsizes

—rights himself.

Grace II

Grace descended upon me today. A small portion,
and somewhat fleeting as she always is.

But quite enough, as she also always is.
So I wept. A little bit, I mean, as I drove my car

through the beautiful world.

I think maybe I wept for the beauty
of beautiful worlds. Or for how she gives

in abundance to requests
never asked. What would I know about it?

Except that she's gone and I'm still here.

A silly something-or-other,
singing softly and not quite in key, gliding

through trees and bees and songs
of birds

on freshly washed streets

in a rain that never fell
that is pouring in me.

A Moment's Excerpt Among the Myriad

Birds! A roaming band of small and pleasant
songbirds has just filled the branches

outside my room.

They tremble
like distant stars upon the barren twigs

and boughs. Today, I am hopeful
and call them angels,

packets of light in transport

beneath a flurry of wings. Each one puffed out
in tender rebellion

against the edges of this world.

Overwhelmed by the sheer gladness
of sunlight and feathers, one suddenly bursts

into song. But the others do not sing.
Perhaps no one is supposed to sing?

But still, there is this one
who just can't help himself.

So he sings again.

Perhaps the Aliens

I picture them thus,
as long sagacious beings

who nod slowly and slowly blink, as ones
who understand, moving like liquid

with their long and lucent hands,

the porcelain hands, nimbused and aglow.
And I picture what hands like these

might do on me. Hands like moons
to lift the massive ocean of failures

from my rigid brittle frame. The kinks, the knots,
the calcified traumas, all pulled taut

and straight like chains, like chains

snapping the whole way up. And the steam
of release. And the sigh, the universal *ahhhhhh* . . .

And then what would I be? What radiance
without this weight? What body

too light to walk? Just touch and go, touch

and go across the glassy floor.
It's true, I've never seen them,

but this is how I want them to be
because it seems I never fully heal.

When I walk the deserts by night,
I'll sometimes cock an eye at the stars,

select and say *That one. Yes, that one will do* . . .
which cues me that it's getting late

because I'm talking to myself again

about spaceships and benefic beings
from other worlds, doing for me

what I must do myself. So I pack it
up for home, shake my head and smile

which also has some healing virtue.

Andromeda

It's a misty night tonight,
she must be taking her bath.

Sprawled in the glory of absolute zero,

she draws the rinse in lakes of ether
the length of her gliding thighs.

The constellations rise and fall,
lap over the basin rim

and stream to the floor of the sky.

She leans her head to a side
and wrings the stars from her hair.

Tonight the centuries between us
seem small and manageable.

Her image rocks on the wide water
of my upturned eyes. Two brief stars

logging on just to say I'm here.
Sending now.

Enough.

I'm all too full of stars.

Acknowledgments

The Iowa Review "Event" (appeared as "Title Poem")
between "Andromeda"
Glyphs "Desert Poem"
Riverbend "River" (appeared as "The Kasilof")

INTRODUCTION

Things call to us; persons call to us; emotions call to us; insights call to us. The world is constantly on-call. Poets, artists and reflective individuals are asked to be evocatively present to such callings. One learns that the particulars of the world call on/to us constantly; they wish to be heard, seen, tasted, felt, enjoyed and suffered. Any creative person is on call, waking or sleeping, because dreams have their own voice and tone in their way of beckoning us to the work.

The above observations are predicated on one belief: we are always understanding the world and ourselves in relation to it by analogy. The world shows us its phenomenal face, but there is something else present as well, invisible but palpable. All forms of art are creative gestures to uncover the deeper correspondences that hold the world together and give all of its parts a coherent form to be comprehended. Each of us has a need to myth-make and myth-shape in our effort to give arrangement to what may remain simply an event in our lives.

Creative acts are courageous instances of one stepping out to glean and give formative expression to what peers through the appearance of things and wants us in the process to meet it part-way, half-way and sometimes all-the-way. An inner animated life of things, of people, of energies we sense that uncovers and informs our own hidden qualities, are what poets strive to shape into a coherent expression to be shared and worked by others. But first the poet must find and have a place in the world, a place perhaps of solitude, from which s/he sees, a poetic perspective unique to the individual creator, the poet. Martin Heidegger furthers this idea when he writes: "we are to think of the nature of poetry as a letting-dwell, as a—perhaps even *the*—distinctive kind of building. If we search out the nature of poetry according to this viewpoint, then we arrive at the nature of dwelling" (213).

This volume of Craig's and my poems are creations of insistent attempts by the inner life of things to be heard, through the words themselves, their arrangements on the page and the fields of interactive relationships they may engender between you, reader, and the poem. At the same time, each of our poems reflects our own way of dwelling, of knowing and of shaping—a *poiesis* of intent and of creation. Each may be seen as an instant in time, an indirect and partly opaque slant of life to arouse your own curiosity as you pilgrimage through each one. We hope they may at times touch your innate impulse to wonder:

- What do these words arouse in me?
- What does this image or these images want to grab hold in me and lead me gently out of my familiar field of apprehending and judging the world?
- What other fields of awareness are opened to me when things of the world, including ideas, feelings, perceptions, bodily senses, prejudices, points of view lead me to another way of seeing and knowing what is around and in me?
- What other set of analogies—metaphors, symbols, likenesses—"as-ifs"—enrich my ordering of the world or, perhaps help me to reorder my understanding along different corridors of discernment?

We each may be organized around a particular set of beliefs that guide us, simply out of habit, but we are not condemned to remain in such a morass for a lifetime. Perhaps the familiar framed one's vision in such a narrow but safe way that one could not venture out from it into the often terrifying and troubling place called "Risk Something." I like the short but profound work by Jane Hirshfield as she meditates on poetry's nature: "Poems, if they are good at all, hold a knowledge elusive and multiple, unsayable in any other form. . . . poetic speech escapes narrowing abstraction and reification as richly as does life itself" *(Hiddenness, Uncertainty, Surprise* 36, 37). Indirection becomes its most satisfying and mysterious medium.

One of our most prolific and original American poets, Emily Dickinson, framed poetry this way in 1863:

> Tell all the truth but tell it slant —
> Success in Circuit lies
> Too bright for our infirm Delight
> The Truth's superb surprise
> As Lightning to the Children eased
> With explanation kind
> The Truth must dazzle gradually
> Or every man be blind —

Her brilliance rests in encouraging us to take an ancillary route and be surprised by what we grasp through indirection and by the slow unfurling of Truth over time. So reread these poems; let them work on you as you work them in whatever way your own mythic self chooses to engage the unfamiliar. Our personal myth hinges, quite simply, on what and to what degree we generously let the world enter and what we are conditioned and therefore convinced, from whatever history or emotional shell, to keep out.

On the lawn of our souls or on the mat resting in front of our front door we are free to put out a sign: "No Trespassing" or "Welcome." We do hope the welcome mats are more numerous and pronounced than the sign that forbids anyone or anything new from entering your proper(ty) format. If mythic seeing is mythic being, then the power of poetry is to reengage and reform your beliefs or at least put some notions out for further reflection.

When I sat with my journal recently, I did what I do each morning: I dwell with an attitude of openness and wait without preconditions for what wishes to be remembered from yesterday. From somewhere in what I was recollecting, the following pushed itself into consciousness:

To marrow and to marrow
And to marrow
Works these petty bones into a
Fullness of femured futures.

Rather than questioning them or seeking their meaning, like a faithful scribe I copied what was offered. They became the substance of a haiku that appears in this volume. Some play on remembering yesterday suddenly created a toe-hold in tomorrow that then found a rich analogy in to marrow—and I let it in.

One of my favorite poets as well as a Buddhist scholar, Jane Hirshfield, who I cited above in one of her other books on poetry, wrote on the poetic imagination: *Ten Windows: How Great Poems Transform the World.* She cites many of the world's finest poets and gives us a constant feast of her own thoughts on poesy. Early on she describes a journal entry of Gerard Manley Hopkins dated 24 February 1873. It is an elegant prose description of snow's drifts and wind impressions that lets us see snow anew.

We read the passage and begin to slip into a reverie, so rich are its associations. Then she asks us to meditate on one of Hopkin's sentences: "Chance left free to act falls into an order as well as purpose" (5). Hirshfield suggests that his rich yet simple description "could only have been written by a person in love with close observation, one who sees with the whole body, and also with the senses of emotion and mind" (5).

Both Craig and I hope some of our poems will, on occasion:

- Awaken you to a fresh way of seeing.
- Encourage you to write a response to one or another of our creations with a poem of your own.
- Instill in you a fresh appreciation for words and for the miracle of language itself.
- Alter your participation of the most ordinary things and events around a richer emotional, even spiritual, response to the ordinary.
- Nourish some part of you desperately hungry and thirsty to be filled, perhaps as sustenance for your spirit.

Finally, I like how Hirshfield describes the intention of a poem: "It is the enactment of an orientation to something that does not yet exist" (11). Hence, a poem's "as-if" angle on something we thought we knew—now breaks into newness and allows for a more inclusive awareness as the gifted consequence of a larger and more complex way of knowing. We hope you see the world and your place in it anew through our creations and allow yourself to dwell there, at least for the time it takes the poem to infiltrate.

Dennis Patrick Slattery

References

Dickinson, Emily. *Poems by Emily Dickinson*. Edited by Mabel Loomis Todd and T.W. Higginson. Boston: Little, Brown, 1912.

Heidegger, Martin. *Poetry, Language, Thought*. Trans. Albert Hofstadter. New York: Harper Collins, 2001.

Hirshfield, Jane. *Ten Windows: How Great Poems Transform the World*. New York: Knopf, 2015.

---. *Hiddenness, Uncertainty, Surprise: Three Generative Energies of Poetry*. Tarset, Northumberland, 200

SELECTED POEMS OF
DENNIS PATRICK SLATTERY

Dedicated to Tim Donohue, Don Carlson, Dan Canalos, Dan
Derdeyn, Robert Palmer and Jennifer Leigh Selig
and to the poetic muses that inspire each of you.

Night Life

Something pithy perhaps
like a late night serenade
strummed and sung
just above a whisper
for her ears only
A song like contraband
hustled across borders
where no wall or fence
has yet been built
He knows the cadence she prefers
the rhythm that touches her insides
and yes, the moon must be full
so the music can hit its mark
be remarkable
Then love can wash up
behind the notes and engulf
them both
and the blue guitar.

Below the Covers

They enter across the pillow
From the left with insistent shards
Of history or the anticipated destruction
Of an event coiled to occur
Head resting on a blue surf, they skim
In at me wave after wave of real scenes
That soured the deck of the present
With old wounds
Scars that suppurate or a future
Already fixed because I've caused
Its edges to curl into a curse.

Nothing good here but sheets of time
Or a photo of my mother's graduation gown
Smeared with the scat from a raccoon living
In the eaves of the garage.
No, that's read, not imagined
So is the other thing being left out
Where does the pain even begin when
The hand is poised like a knife cutting the
Air?
But this other story is different.
Arrested at the airport because you waved down
a patrol car to tell them you
did not like the odor in the rent car
you just unlocked so you opened the trunk
and found the smelly source
a corpse in repose
submerged in its own compost.

But you are suspect so they cuffed you
And pushed you into the back seat. Your
Pleas to use the bathroom ignored
You wet your pants and soiled their cruiser

Under arrest now for defacing public property
That's the kind of stubborn montage that abuses
Sleep and soils a good pair of slacks and now
You have a record.

You missed your chance to shout for help. Everything
Has grown twice as large as it need be
Should be.
I have lost all contact with the feel of
My skin; like me it waits in the back seat
For the next story. Wash the pillow case
And leave it blank as a sheet of paper
Then demand the officer step on it.

Letters Scent
For The Past

Where did the letters go?
They all vanished
at least two maybe three
shoeboxes filled with scented
envelopes that brought you
back in a skiff of emotions.
And what did they say
those folded sails of scented
pages that I looked for
yearned after each day when
school was done and I rode
my bike home or ran the
full distance?
There on the kitchen table a
heap of mail I sifted through
with quick hands seeking the
scent and when none was
found I, crushed, wadded up
like a discarded page
sulked to my room or
when the space was too close
drove myself outside and
ran the streets to put distance
between my aching stomach
and tomorrow's mail.
I sought too much from life
at fourteen and compressed
by disappointment as if I had
no me without the sealed fragrance
Of you of your words
telling me I am missed
that I am loved.
All the wilderness of words in tennis shoe

boxes, shoes that run and tell—
they are all gone, worn through
descending somewhere
deep below me
in some landfill perhaps.
The letters littered like seeds
still pushing up in my soiled
past
offering hope—scented and
so neatly folded, like you
terrible to recollect for what
it opens inside me—
like the slice of a letter opener
across the flap you glued closed
with your sweetly glazed tongue
sticky now and so full
of desire
so edgy with joy
so scented with Hope.

God's Erotic Presence

Create a clean heart in me, O God.
Renew in me a steadfast spirit.
~Psalm 50

At Vespers we give thanks
and pray to the Lord for His
bounties.
A retreatant asks that we thank
the Creator for the orange gold
plashed sunset that ignited the
Pacific ocean from our great heights
in the mountains of Big Sur.
Ok, such a prayer is surely worthy.

But what about this: in the evening before prayers
I stood on the tidy porch of my hermitage
called Kairos at just the right moment
and admired two trees subtly swaying
 gently in the nodding night air
that my own Kairos began to sway in response.

I gripped the railing unafraid and felt
the rhythm of the earth answer the sway
of the cottonwoods; then a hundred pheasants
detonated out of the foliage
by the tiny road in one flutter
of feathers around the swayed splendor
of trees that pulsed the entire world in motion
a movement of spirit crafting elegant shapes
of the day's declining de-light.
Such an orchestra of divine profusion in matter
raced through me in wonder.
The self-contained rhythm of motion before me
eclipsed the sun's daring beauty.
I think the trees' barely perceptive tilting fore

- 91 -

and aft dared me to gamble on God's seductive dance
in the leaves that decided as one
to come along for the ride.
They too are part of poetry's enthused insistence.
Is it any wonder?

Haikus

Our cat scratched the door
Lightning strikes each of her paws
Once more freedom purrs

Snow crystals cling fast
Doves circle frosty snow banks
Spring winks to the sun

A scarf hides cold bones
Winter sits atop stiff trees
A wren's wings rustle

Solitude rises
Sleep hides behind rustling veils
Winter dawn flashes

Yesterday vanished
My journal casts a wide net
Now tomorrow sees

Dark days behind me
Martin Luther King in front
Sky scattered by birds

Fog wants to be mist
Sun seeks shadows by a tree
Now the darkness smiles

Love poetry's plight
It hugs its useless life
Words scatter when heard

To marrow and to marrow and
To marrow
Works these petty bones
Into fullness of
Femured futures

Real Work that Matters

Finding water for the thirsty
              or nourishment for those starved
                      from the violence of
            conformity.
Not the endless line of lunches
            in retirement—no
                the work that music creates
                    that mimics life in its leathery
creaking interior.
             The work of exploring how
                Telemachos enters the dark myth
                    of origins when he searches
not for his father Odysseus
            but for the stories scattered in his wake
              a way to own his own history.
                THAT work endures
has a shape and a certain aroma.
            It smells like life itself glad
              in hours of repose—to still
                have the gnawing energy of
resolve.
            It does not matter if
              this pursuit ever waves back.
              I can live without the gesture
but not without the purpose.

When Mending Migrates

The moon a sickled silence
    carries its white light into
        my early morning window
to illuminate the title of
    a poem:
        "I Watched a Snake."

Something, perhaps
    a tattered part of myself
        or the larger world is mended
when the moon migrates
        to the snake's silver scape.

Are these moment-events
    all around us seeking to amend
        what peers from the
    sleeve of a splint?

Noticing is by nature
    the beginning of an amendment
        so intentional in silence
    like the moon a soft sickle
    of repose—

Suspended, amended and
    befriended by the blackness
        stitching the moon snake
    into a spiral
        a pattern of sorts
    that mimics my own return.

Deep Enough?

These words—their aspect was obscure—
I read/ inscribed above a gateway, and I said:
"Master, their meaning is difficult for me."
Inferno III

Is my reading deep enough?
Can I attend to the pilgrim's
sinister descent where stench
assaults the eyes and the shades
crisp in scabbed skin
rend the ears into scratched awakenings?

What form might Virgil
virgin of the underworld assume
his dark shape and clothed
poetic pose wrapping arms
around his naïve charge
pushes him along
through loiter-free zones
echoing moans of remorse.

The naked truth groans in a chorus
of demented laments.
No birds fly through gummy air.
Mistakes in life cling with miniature
fury to everlasting nows
pock marks in eternity.

A river to their left courses
hot bubbles of blood;
shades breach to the surface
chunks of meat in a stew that
know their own end:

Consistent
Insistent
Resistant

Fictional Figurals

The body is a device to calculate
The astronomy of the spirit.
~Rumi, *Selected Poems*

Ishmael goes to sea
to become oceanic
Huck climbs aboard his raft
to discover his own river bed
Marlowe sits Buddha-like on the bow of a
Steamer seeking his own invisibility
Kurtz skulks along the lapping
river shore hoping to heed
his own horror
Gilgamesh dives deep into
the lake of snakes to fathom the death
of himself.

All become fictional figures
of aligned facts.
Dante plunges deep into
river Lethe to disremember
who he might become.

Watery whorls keep each
who floats
upright.
Visit the deep on your own
or be dragged there in your
sleepiest soft spot.
Either way, you are destined.

Remain in the water
long enough
fresh or bruised
and a halo will form

around your feet.
Such is the consequence
of your patience with
the spirits of the deep.

Narrative Longing

A storied life is not a sorry life.
"Can I," he wondered,
"back out of a story
into the ground of experience
that rises to a quivering narrative
full of its own desire to be told?"
The woods in back of our house
darken when the sun is highest.
It cannot penetrate the shades of things
or the shadows of beings.
Only a vignette is sharp enough
to pierce obscurity's tender reeds.
Only the tight line of a plot transfers the energy
on which a natural glows rests quietly.
Can he separate the story
from the storied?
Is it any wonder streams find
other grooves to shine in?
Other truths to rise from?
Not real—only true.
Let the dark woods form the words
that led him from bewildered shadows
to the other side of the story's shore—
the side not told,
the side still longing.

I See the Narrow Gauge

I see the narrow gauge
separate light from memory.
The spiral turn of a thought
when it wanders toward insight
bearing down on a passage from *Inferno*
until it loosens its hold on a secret
after seven hundred years.
A point of view appears
as a character in a three-part perspective.
A first glance at the splendor of a secret
when pressed secretes revelations of beauty.
So does a form grow inside a chambered nautilus
whorl by whorl by shimmering degrees.
In the flicker appears a new function
without blemish, calm in itself
like moonlight—unbroken.
Let's dare to take a walk
At midnight.

Words Dry Out

Where goes what withers
to be refreshed?
The heat of a day's longing
is enough to sap all moisture
from the stems of things.
Withering roots where ecstasy
grows upward in a forest
without fear? Loosen your hold
on dry sticks when combustion
is near. Fear makes deserts of
our destinies.

Moisten your lips with olive oil.
Take pains to live close to a well.
Follow the white porcelain of mist.
Push fear to the curb and the stories
that wet its plots.

Danger in the details of a
negative narrative
dry the soul to a brittle cloth
bereft of blessings.
Seek still waters and
awaken.

Struggling Toward Form

What should the poem do?
What can still be saved?
~Jorie Graham, "The Marriage"

This morning with only a white candle lit
I look back again and again at yesterday
and see through a glass vessel
tinted blue at what didn't happen,
wanted to, had the right balance of
desire and purpose to become matter
to matter to someone but failed to join
the line of small insects crawling across
the space of time shaping themselves
from a string of events into memories
to a convincing plot that created
the night so today could blister forth,
become a patterned set of thoughts
mixed into an elixir with schedules,
appointments, chance encounters
and barely visible inklings of
tomorrow's joyful promises.

I fear that none of them will make it
into print
to be wondered at as if
they were happening right now.
I remain open to their rough outline.

New Camaldoli Hermitage

Foraging in the scent
Of one flower fair
Not daffodils or dandelions
But violets through her hair
The smell of musk against the
Placid ocean blue
Fills the monastery walls with
Prayers that grace the evening dew

So high above Pacific curls in
Contemplation sound—not
One bird can hear the clock
In hermitage resound.

Penitent be, after vespers five
Seek the dead one who slipped
The cross to tender mercies thrive.

Christmas Gifts

"I have all these boxes to mail," he says.

His voice is pleasant and chatty in the long line to mail his packages. He jokes with the woman standing behind him holding four small boxes. She is short, wearing a worn hoodie and struggling to balance her Christmas packages.

"Yes, after these I'll go home and bring in six more this afternoon to mail."

"Oh," he says to something she asks him; I cannot hear what it is.

"One day is pretty much the same as all the others. I just live a few miles from here, in Canyon Lake. We found a good deal on the house we liked so we bought it." All in that order.

I am next in line. I step up to mail my two parcels. I think of the conversation that has now dissolved in front of me.

I want to send a book to the man whose days are all the same. But really, could words in a book of poems, say, be of service to him? Would he even bother to read it?

I wonder if his days have turned into concepts while he was not paying attention; or all the wrinkles of each one ironed out so there is no marking one day from another. The days, now bled of life, are no longer able to shine as

Particular

Peculiar

Laced with wonder.

In the wake of presence I am awakened to something not there before: to pay close attention to the creases and rumples in each day, to note where a button is missing, a collar frayed—all with their own personal delights shining through the ordinary. No, that IS the ordinary—a quickening sense of the quirky quotidian.

Mailing gifts to others, I am gifted by this man, an oracle of the ordinary.

Undergo the Treatment

"You'll be just fine" the specialist said.
"No dying on my watch."
"Just watch" Death says
turning meat to mush;
surgeons rush to prescribe
to treat who cannot face the failure
or even the pulse of defeat.
A long death after a short life
ties no bows, completes no knot.

But what if I favor Death
over the malignant life your care
ushers in?
"Whose Death is it?" I propose
to the intern wearing latex skin.
And more—the vibrant life
pulsing in joy within.
Your treatment is a
cheatment meant to prolong
a deadly life.
Something backward here
inside out
what purpose in the struggle to
keep us alive when only death
nature's farewell
seems to be the only prize?
Work these last breaths taken in form
not through pumps that deny
the chest from slowing to
its own arrest.

Recall the will's clear refrain:
"Do not resuscitate"
just ease the pain.

Give up your treatments
tests and probes
so unprepared are you
to the deeper throes
of life's desire to end the rout
allowing Death finally to win out.

Accept the fate that lies within
that dying coils beneath the skin.
Comfort those who seek their end
by living fully toward the goal:
Amen.

The Earth Moved For Two Days[*]

He gathered the elders and
spread before them photos
of a dozen rifles pointing
in unison into the massive pit
where bodies stood or slumped
and looked up into the black holes
of rifle barrels already
spewing their hot bullets
from eye to mind.
A mother in the foreground
clinging to her infant
 ordered to hold the child
in front of her to be executed
with grand efficiency.
A single bullet passes with
heated indifference through the soft
flesh of life full of anticipation
and promise into the mother
holding despair with both hands
in a chaos of crushed feathers.
"We all came out to watch,"
remembers a village woman in
her 80s when images buried in
the hard earth surfaced in
united memories after
seventy years of fetal forming.

---

[*]In the territory of Moldova in the former Soviet Union 75 years after the
fact, a French catholic priest, Patrick Desbois, resurrected mass graves
and collective memories of Jewish families herded into earthen holes,
shot, and covered over. Many survivors were still alive. He interrogates,
using archived images, those who were only 8 or 9 years old when they
witnessed the mass murders.

"What I remember most was that
after soil was shoveled over
dozens of our Jewish
neighbors, the earth continued
to move for two days."
Perhaps an arm reached out
from the terrified dirt
futilely resisting what it was
expected to do: hide the
dying and the dead from sight.
But what the shivering earth
failed to achieve within
its own limits
was to cover the living
who could only peer into
the rising pit; they too
were wounded and dying
or else standing in mud the
color of their own death.
Their memories bullet-ridden
their arms reaching toward
the shuddering loosely-packed
pit pleading to those suffering
in their final minutes, hours, days
now resting quietly having
survived the horror of hate and
Holocaust,
redemption no longer
possible.
Or for compassion hidden
in the deep foundations of
an idea only now
pushing up from the loam
yearning to reach even a
still birth.
Anything would be better than
having to look out one's filmy

window at the stirring earth
beckoning to them, hoping
for them
to return before
all quaking ceased and
the earth resumed her
deadly stillness.

Wandering

Out of the forest
    Of a cramped necessity
I become only what I am:
    Being roiling toward Becoming

    A paradox of purposes
Propels me fore and aft.
    Life is continuous rhythm
Between home and wandering.

No one is not a wonder
    To behold
However one denies it.

Freedom bewilders
    Only when we begin.
I hold the love of you
    In sacred trust
And love myself in tandem.

    Only those are free
Who wander in delight
    Of the ordinary and
Originary without end.

Ask then: what shall I assent to?
    What shall I ascend to?
When you can cease fighting yourself
    You are already turned
In the right direction.

    Home: where the heart resides
And the hearth warms us
    From within.

"Yes" and "No" are polar ice caps
　　We trudge between for a lifetime.
The goal of course is
　　Within the frozen part of our heart.

　　Do not cease the experiment
In the few years we are given.
　　To be homeward bound is
Freely chosen, freely gifted.
　　　　Go now, move to the next station.

Haikus

Comfort
No wind stirs in me
Sails sway in the harbor lights
Life stops in my soul.

Turbulence
Turbulence invites me
Run into the wind with joy
Let the rudder go

Face It
One place frightens me
Yesterdays graze tomorrows
Run towards the phantoms

Loosening
My ground slides beneath
Nothing to grip any more
Freedom finds moonlight

Tightening
I smell groundlessness
now increase my grip on life
the red sky set

The Ardor of Order

Uncertainty inhabits all poems.
~Jane Hirshfield, *Ten Windows*

Begin with your own story
    plotted by the gloves of
Enthusiasm—
    Rising in the morning on the
other side of the chasm
    turns a page in the project of
a story not sold
    but one that yearns to be bold
with eloquence in elegiac mode
    the spiral that speech bends toward
to shape a coiling tale.

Once you climbed a cyclone fence
    and punctured the palm of your hand.
Years later you walked on stage to
    accept a degree with the wound
of that childhood grip.
    Narrative thickened at the birth
of your son—the body in turmoil
    pushing life straight into the world
the world into circling life.
Grazing through books, you found
    an unturned stone
peaked underneath and wrote
    your own history absent
rhyme or season.

    Published
it wore the lace of an index.
    Tending later to the rows of
spinach and dill

garlic and radish
on knees scarred decades ago
      you kept the earth at the hearth
of your story
      rooting identity close to cabbage
and cucumber
      circling the seasons in delight
in the folds of a life
      free of lies. Tasting of mint
garnishing a plot that will not repeat
      only spiral back to shade the future.
Done. Unamended
      past rough drafts and beyond all edits.
Freely you accepted its order; with the
      same ardor that coaxed you skyward
then dropping to the other side of a wounded
      fence handily conquered.
More than enough for a story.

Silence First and Always

There is a way between voice and presence
where information flows.
~Rumi, *Selected Poems*

Silence first and always before speech.
    Let the air be still
  in the dark hours
    before the lamp is lit;
   chase the dreams into corners.
What form this day will take
    cannot be otherwise.
Today I will say what needs to be said
      on this day only: part of a story,
  a phrase held in the still pocket of my soul,
a forgotten noun. Utter it now
    or hold its peace for another year.
Urgency does not mean
  a flushed face or a rushed phrase;
      speech can drown in its own commotion.
When Presence arrives you will know it
   by its fabric texture and timing.
Foolish or wise—just show up!
  Words will gather soon enough.
    The converse is also true.

Pulleys and Wheels

> The way things work
> is that eventually
> something catches.
> ~Jorie Graham, "The Way Things Work"

Even the day has levers and pulleys
       I dive through the maze of mechanics
    stopping here, adjusting
wheels there
       splitting my time between
   a red STOP button
at the top of a rectangle
       a green GO button below it
    dangling from a vertical cord.

Keep the destruction clear
       for the moment when a quick decision
    insists one grab the rectangle
swinging from the car's ceiling and
       push the right button without looking.

Above, a large boom makes its way
       across the factory sky
    advancing along the route I'm driving
silent on iron rails stretching along a life.

I manage the myth that is its energy
       its entelechy, its entropy.

Precise measure keeps
       mechanics of motion from
    dismantling and showering the streets
below with nuts and bolts of
             uncertainty.

Smiling Moon

You can climb
Back up a stream of radiance to the sky.
~Robert Frost, "The Master Speed"

How many times in the early hours
of my study
have I looked up and out to
the night sky and saw the smile of the moon
those sharp-pointed horns
riding the silver of reflected sunlight.

Already it has moved behind the branches
of the live oak
that keeps it company now in its leaves
a thick branch and behind the grinning
captured joy of the moon a pink sky
dimly echoes the first flush of
Saturday morning.

Such a series of spectacles
just beyond the book I read
the notes I make and
the lunacy of life's gifts.

Fading in the aromas that
the morning air brings, a gentle warning:
This day is not to be   laid   waste.

Branching Out

Early Saturday morning trimming back
small trees from the wooden fence
out front along the property line.
No breeze, thick Texas August air
as I settle into the swagger of sweat.

Something releases in me when
I see the branches from around the
slats of wood; they fall startled
to my feet. The air is moist with
cutting back, opening the slats of
the long fence to the open air,
free of the pressure of wood.

Some renewal fidgets in me.
The pile of severed branches grows
around my walking boots. It is joy
I have not felt in a life too cluttered
with projects that choke the wood
of my own boundaries.
Joy sighs among the trees.

My wife drives up and parks in the garage.
She walks out to see my slim trees breathing
fresh air unfettered.
I, light now, feel her warmth in
the sun-streaked air
and the trees, so uncluttered now
begin to grow new branches around us
and another story finds a small space
to take root with no fenced limits
to discourage its surrender.

Writing's Erasure

Friend, you are my collaborator in this venture.
~Mark Strand, "The Monument"

In no time
each sentence I
read or write
becomes a memory.
Slippered in the morning
it is less than a beaten brogan
by midday
and a worn sock by sunset.
Then how do we remember
with enough elegance
to fill a shoebox?
Lethe limps along behind
every line I linger over
holding to a fresh start
in the shadow of erasure.
My day suffers with the
wounds of deletion,
my lines limn every crease.

Walking Out of Water

Shed the skin of war Cacciato believed
up in the high country out of
Viet Nam
"If war won't leave me,
then I'll. . . .
shed the bayonet, ammo pouch
dreams that terrified—the whole
backpack of misery up, up
the slippery clay trail, skin
peeled off by a dull knife."

The jaundiced world of woe
tilting the crucifixion resting
on a lower lip,
the stunted prayers of a
pocket-sized New Testament.

Cacciato hurling toward high ground
reducing his load when he
paused to oversee torments of
jungle shivers, futures napalmed
into despair and death shattered
by one malignant bullet.
Up and over the crazed haze
over dazed days when new souls
once grazed in pastures of plenty.

They Were Carried by the Wind[†]

Their bodies so light
like kites without strings
shirts and skirts rustling
hard to remain aloft
miles above.
The earth looked up at them
first with indifference
then with a yearning petrified
out of the field grass
to welcome them with
fragile limbs.
But the winds aloft
refused to let them fall
so fast
so they floated above the debris
of their parents' bodies
too heavy to resist the flow
of gravitas after the
explosion thrust them
beyond metal and fuel
beyond all distractions
save one.

[†] http://www.newyorker.com/magazine/2015/09/28/the-avenger
Ken Dornstein, a documentary film maker, whose brother David died in
the December 1988 airline crash of Pan Am 103, has for years been
researching who was responsible for the bombing of the plane that killed
all aboard. One can read the *New Yorker* article above. As Dornstein
showed the article's author, Patrick Radden Keefe, his rooms with photos
and other materials related to the flight, he drew the author's attention to
some pins on a map: "Motioning at a scattering of pushpins some
distance from the rest, he said, 'They were the youngest, smallest children.
If you look at the physics of it, they were carried by the wind.'"

After the initial violence
the young souls
were shot into the thin air
too anemic to breathe.
But they were close to those
who loved them most
till size selected the
small ones to sail the currents
farther and longer than
their elders—more mattered
than they.
In my memory I prayed
they were not allowed
to think any of these
thoughts.
But only to clear the trees
houses and towns to secure
a place of repose coming
to greet them now faster
in desire
quicker, fleeting even
rushing to an end of land fill
and then serene, clear of torched
homes and villagers burning
from the apocalypse in paint
and loose chairs
tattered seat belts only a
nauseous dream.
Settling now, the winds
calming their fury of rage
over the blackened hearts that
knew not one of their first names
nor what they dreamed of becoming.

Story's Line

Writing and anger go together.
~James Hillman, "Writing"

What do I move closer to
       that threatens
   to end my life?
What grieving draws me to stories
       that should have been left
   in a plastic bag decades ago

like that battle where words
       became spears or the time
   the indifference of another
when I reached out like a child
       someone had forgotten
   at the grocery store or car wash

for anybody to pull me in somewhere
       anywhere really or the unkind look
   from a stranger who knew me for
as long as the eye needs to blink twice.
       I would recall other stories
   of rich moments when someone
beamed at me: "You brightened my day!"
       I had no clue what had passed between us
   with enough space to receive such
a benediction.
So go out now; ramble and play
   and speak and smile at whoever
       glances your way.
Surely souls by you seek
   their own solace; your remembrance
       may sustain their life.
Purpose frolics before them
   and grace enters as a thrice-bold
       tale.

Wayfarer

the idiom in you, the why—
~Jorie Graham, "Soul Says"

Sing your song in the idiom
    that distills you—
        bang your drum in the idiom
that thrills you.
If you find a story that catches
    at the shards of your
        worn plot
chew it up and in.
    Let its spangles carry you
        until yesterday freezes over.
Sense the cycle of your quivering myth
        dilating the mouth
    that utters and the ears
that shudder but still listen.

Your voice slyly hidden
        your vowels arising unbidden
    describe the best parts of you.
At this stage in life
    silence is olden
        patience only beholden.

Be seen then and
    Not be herd.
        Cling to your own practice.

Two Forms of Life

Awe is the salve that will heal your eyes.
~Rumi, *Selected Poems*

A man with a gray face woke
With a keen thirst wanting after desire.
Stillness is so far on the other side of
The dream he floated in last night.

An old man with a white face
Fell one morning into a
Critical morass.
His old terrain offered few options.
No matter—within the slide show
Of a shallow life
He complains it is someone's fault
But his words fall around him
In hopeless heaps of old snow.

Melodic Lines

Music prints the air in sheets
enough to cover the path
Adele walks on: notes on her soles
and lyric lines limn her thoughts

Between the aches of an uncertain hour
and the long chords of lament
glass melodies lag
without the rhythm of lonely
parts seeking one another again
in time after time.

Yes and Gnaw
For Jorie Graham

     Something here wishing
to be born
only at first a gnawing sense
then a gnaw into knowing
the nibble quick of response to
a crease in life
or the yaw and gnaw of
the rats deep in the ship's
listing hold.
     Pause when least in
the gnaw; easy now.
The size of the bite is
a seizure on history
beneath the moon
always glazing the night
air with sounds from a
 fool's rush.
     Find the place of the detail
in chains
tugging on metal lashed
to the leg; now outward
turn, only the heaving break
of history circling each bone
between ligatures of
past---future.
     Take your time; bite
down slowly on the
quick wit of a detail
long forgotten
moving through the in-wit
of a life lived in haze
the days a blur of
dogs' legs: run past

the past
where the fog lays over
the terrain of time
yet suspended
never ended in the broken
fierce of now.

What Still Teaches Me

> Don't wash a wound with blood.
> ~Rumi, "Shadow and Light Source Both"

Rumi: What hurts you blesses you.
Me: Awe is the leaf of a tree
fallen on your vision.
Awe is the way
through the enchanted familiar.

The full moon at 4 a.m.
teaches me silence
teaches me song.
The sun at midday
riots through the window
to show me when I am wrong.

Stay with the moonlight.
It is sunlight without sound.

Sutures

Here is the skin of days in the one hand of God.
~Jorie Graham, *The Dream of the Unified Field*

where in the catacombs
do you find the shards
where cracks reign
beating along on bare feet
through the ancient patterns?
those you know:
where people open
where myth changes shape
when she finds everything closed.
even the ground shows cracks
made by swelling waves.
out into the open
just consider the gap between us.
ground swells of loneliness
that resist mending

forgive—one painful stitch at a time.
keep the finger out.
use it as your needle leaving a trail of cat gut
a long strained transparent line of hurts.

Not in Service

When abandoned words rust
corrode
lose all elastic give.
Sentences too begin to dissemble
disassemble.
Bolts and nuts
holding words together
dismantle
or freeze so hard against each other
they lose all meaning
no longer worth mentioning.

Others can be sprayed
lightly with WD-40
or more shining bright
with the lubricant of use
or the hammer of metal.
A plow left idle rusts from the
outer edges in.

But cutting through the earth
turning over clods to the sun it shines
in a shimmer of use.
So we must keep
our blade in the soil.
The soul too rusts over with neglect.
Beliefs lock in corrosive columns.
Forgive no one dull and
Without conviction.
No more glittering in sunlight
arthritic in non-motion
a life stuck in place
slowly evaporating
in the indifferent curve of the air.

Better to be nubbed and shining
then long dull and useless.
But is any space left for a sharp poem
to split the dirt in our own field?

Patience

A slammed door
is impatient with
key and latch.
Patience has an odor
that soothes the
Dandelion wine in
your blood—

It can see out in
soft gauze without
the wildness in the eye.

Sit outside on a rock
that lets you see all around.
Patience is a panorama
where nothing is not
noticed.
Beneath the filaments
of a vast forest
the energy of patience
professes each stem
leaf and trunk.

Without it nothing
grows into its own stature.
Patience pats the head of hurry
and speaks a soothing
"There, there. . . Nevermind"

Patience's claim is always
to be there
Now.
Patience waits with its silent
partner—wonder.
No stopping this pair.

Quiet Rebels

A quiet rebellion in the eyes
rollicking across Texas ranch roads
on lazy mornings misty
with large-eyed deer.
Splendored resistance
like the energy Dante
pushes back with
not ready for the fire
he knows won't burn him
but its licking flames are pain enough.
He recoils into himself
where Beatrice's welcome gleams,
a new sun, a fireball of Grace.
Stepping back now
seems a coward's rhyme
uncertain what to believe
or where to place his time.

Serenity in Likeness

To find in one another
some likeness in history
is unlike the seeing of the many.
Memory singes the past
with its own truths, failures, limits
flimsy to the touch
but fierce in staying power.
Now is the power of our birth, amen.
Cancelled checks scorch money
remembered.
I am unlike you in
dress and dross

And yet—
Below ground we circle slowly
in the same den   the same dim light
of a future undressed
waiting for a proper fitting.
You—a likeness monster
in your ordinary wrap
now find your own solace
where wind whistles in
the cave at dawn.
Similar—yes--like yesterday
But not the same really.

Scattered As-Ifs

I recognized in play the "As if," as the driving
force of aesthetic activity and intuition.
~Hans Vaihinger, *The Philosophy of As-If*

I use the electric blower to scatter
        the startled leaves from
    the front deck, its wood painted
a dark brown highlights
        the fragile tiny Live Oak
    droppings piled this December
morning. They lie in patterns
        I cannot yet discern, each
    a tiny fear.
I lack the proper words for
        such subtle sightings.

The blower raises them as if a
        chorus of locusts up-scattered
    toward the edge of the deck and
beyond, a given instinct of
        final life.
A few soar toward their
        birthplace on a branch just
    above the roof line
but so out of reach
        like those moments when
    I seek the forgotten name
that would assemble an entire
        idea in motion and time
    just out of grasp in
the starlings of appetite.
        Desire-laden
    not enough traction to travel.
Leaves as words

many frayed to death
others parts of scattered sentences
that could explain so much—perhaps
          Origin itself, as if that could be known.

Tomorrow more leaves will
          welcome me on the deck
     when I pass through the front door
toward the garage
          where, standing in wonder
     between truck and motorcycle
what I traveled there to find
          now disconnected, urgent
     in repose to be recollected.
Memory scatters its own leavings
          from door to door.
     Perhaps broom and rake would
prove better utensils for
          gathering and repeating what
     was once a promised story idea
or a code to break the fingers of
          Forgetfulness.
Left to their own pattern
          might all the as-ifs measure
     out a common song to believe in?

When Will You Come to It?

Not at noon or
          just before it or
When it filters towards
                    dusk—
Perhaps too early or
          too late.
The shoreline is a fine
               starting place
   or right where the
                    forest opens
   and closes like your
          heart chambers, in
   synch with something larger
          not yet recognized.
Your movement too
          figures in the
proportion—the measure
   of things and the accuracy
               of your calculus—
   When to push forward
          against custom and
habits that break you a
          little bit each day
against shapes that arrest
          your thought and stop
   all worthy imaginings.
It—knows you already,
   nothing hidden here
   except yourself—in
   clothes that don't fit
and a smile that fails
   to become you—
It waits, however. It
   knows you are not yet

ready
still ill-prepared
    but yearning to respond
    to It
            a lavish program
humming at the heart
    of things
                fully worth
your progress but only if
    you continue to track It.
Travel no farther than
    the sound of your heart's
    rhythm,
ready to rise outside yourself
    to Its insistent vision.

No Thought There

No thought present just being.
   When the sentence appears
      I feel the roilings of apprehension
Just now when the words unfold
   Something ignites, seeks fuel to
      Enlarge, consumes all appetites
Like an idea when some kindling
   Warms its edges.
      Not failing but falling somewhere
Into_____ when life forms on
   Its own like a cluster of leaves in Spring
      Sticky moist and feeling their
Own incomplete unfurling
   Move across the sentence and down
      Through the small white space in its letters
Or in the gaps of space
   When each word breathes on its own.
      It is easy to grieve for a lost clause
      Dependent
         Independent
      But it hardly matters when my eye
Slows to the period
   Beyond which is little to recommend it.
      The end of a world erupts abruptly.
Sometimes—in the early hours of a humid morning
   There is little left to be said or written
      No reason pushes me out of bed.
Silence recommends itself
   Right beside it
      Repose seems wisest
Stories can wait till noon.
   Lavish in shadows
      The sense of things waits
         To bloom.

I have time for it now
Finally.

Only Breath

There is an aperture between voice and presence
where information flows.
In disciplined silence it opens;
with wandering talk it closes.
Breath without words to fill it
invites riches from others' ears.
Gaze without vision or image.
Filling it up is clear seeing.
Taste without food stocks appetite
for the night journey.

Touch without skin warms the sickled moon
aglow in the speckled night sky.
Life without light gains a darkness
that fills in the traumas tomorrow
will bring.
So for today—let go
the outbreath and all that clings
to its vibrant flow.

Completion

Depth started to throb.
~Jorie Graham, *The Dream of the Unified Field*

The painting sits upright
        against the file cabinet
   almost completed; it can't
find the place of finish, a space
        where things are permitted to end.
   No studio for it to be done
signed and touched no more
with thoughts of brush.

It needs a tiny woman
        walking away from the viewer
   with her tiny black dog no larger
than a leaf/just a stain of black
        will bring it to life.
   But no proper space avails
to allow it a final shape
a completion.
The smaller trees in back
        then larger and still larger
   masses of green, mottled trunks in front
stand alone beside one another;
        they smell the loneliness.
   Cezanne can't find his own footing
his easel or canvas stand.
        The asphalt path ribbed
   with shadows of trees we cannot see
because the woman and her dog
        have long passed
        yet remain unpainted.
They want to be there, content to stroll
        as they do in the photograph I paint from.

Some license, surely, but not them
they are not incidental to the life of trees.
I want to see them—after they are painted in
            two figures to ease the gap of loss in depth.
      When the painting is framed and hung
on the bedroom wall, I want to see
            them enjoying the trees
      I painted for their delight as they stroll
by and through the lushness of green.
I wave to their tiny shapes
            meandering on the path, their
      backs to me growing smaller
her dog sniffing a red wildflower
unaware I am behind them
            happily waving brush in hand at their beauty.
      They continue to diminish
            as do I to them
in my blue shirt, like hers
 now almost the same size.
            They never look back

Forty Again

Between similar and
    same
is a cavern of dry ice
    bluish in sunlight

Some of us repel to the stiff
    narrowing crevasse
but descents do not alter
    history's melting cap

My history your memory
    frame themselves
through the shutters
    of the present

Now in my vision a crouching likeness
    poses on steel claws
where you I and others can
    people the same space
in like time when
    Uranos Pluto conjunct

The prompt is sufficient
    for us to recall one another
        delight in fields of insight
here now and for all time

Let's agree to begin with
    the first forty
The next will be similar
    Yes   like yesterday's
but hardly the same

This we can count on.

Read On

Am I more than my story?
Does each day reckon with
that "more" before 8 a.m.
when dreams cease plotting
their twisted scenes into a
confusing weave with the story
I think I will live further today
than yesterday allowed?
The open windows in the
living room
the draped ones in the bedroom
each flutters solace to the
stories recited in
the kitchen or scribed
in the shadows of the study.
If your life is no worse
than the story you
recollect each morning
then will you live long enough
to know in rich detail
how it all turns out?
We can't know for certain
but the way it passes
along the edge of death
its disarming lip
makes me want to read on.

Light the Blackness

Silk must not be compared
with striped canvas.
~Rumi, *The Essential Rumi*

In the middle of a candle
a black wick. Into it a flame
alights.
In the steady cool blackness
light catches and flames.
Light your candle where
you see blackness.
Then your flame will
flicker and bob
flicker and waver
Delighted to be there.

Not Remembered

To think of death as life's
residue animates images
of all the deceased clustering around me
in Dallas, San Luis or down the street
 where we continue to live.
What of the dead mouse in the trap
by the furnace who entered from its
own underworld seeking warmth
on a cold Texas night?

Curious it snapped the trap basted
with a modest dollop of peanut butter.
We heard from the bedroom the metallic
unforgiving ring of steel against wood
then a short struggle behind a closed door
then silence.

Loss, letting go—I carry trap and mouse
to the trash bin. The corpse trails
an odor of a life spent
dark eyes wide open in a final
face-off with surprise and betrayal.

Life carries death to the bin
a sorry cemetery without
rites or glory.

Let someone remember me
I think
so mortality can play without
rancor but denied the
final word.
Death be not proud
in-adamant Dei.

Dream the Prize

Seek what you have
Dive before the watercourse
shrinks into shallows

Find the thread that unravels
back to the shirt you are wearing
Travel south of anger
west of resentment
north of desire and
east of envy—

Find the center of your own
silence
Use every word as if it were
a mud brick you shaped
with your own hands
Stack them carefully—
Celebrate your birthday every
day save the one you were born on

At night, find a bridge to sleep
beneath
Watch for the prize
It will float in the dark silent silk
river just feet from
where you dream

In the morning, bathe
in its glassy silence and feel the
new skin packing you in
like a gold bar swaddled
in blue satin.

Survival: A Prose Poem

One of our three cats—the orange one
that adopted us three years ago
and who we now feed, along with our
two sisters hand-picked from the Humane Society
holdings, disappeared after two neighboring
dogs loose and on the growl
cornered and attacked this furry fluff
of orange.
But she fought back, scratched one of the dogs
on the nose, then disappeared
skipped all meals placed on the front deck
where she liked to dine in solitude.
She would appear at 2 pm each day
from somewhere on our wooded property
always greeting us with a tiny half-squeak
of gratitude.
Four days passed with her absence signaling
to us she was hurt beyond repair
or she lit out for safer surroundings.

On the fifth day I drove my truck into
the garage and remembered another cat,
a stray kitten this time, who found us
perhaps by the scent of our two sisters;
perhaps they drew her in.
She played in the garage, a soft purry
thing, and seemed happy until yet another
stray cat, a more aggressive black male
less generous with the space he claimed
attacked and wounded her.
I found her body, deeply ravished, behind
the garage freezer. We buried her with
great sadness, so young and naïve and
wide-eyed with enjoyment.

Now, I walked to that same place
dreading what I might find again
and peered through sunlight in to the
constricted space between freezer and
garage wall to see a carpet of orange
lying very still. Her hind quarters were
mostly visible.
I was stung with the sense she too had crawled
into the same space to die.

I walked to the freezer's other side and looked
through the darkness to see her face—it was
there, attached to the rest of her—blinking
out at me. I felt a rush of orange joy.
My wife and I coaxed her out with
a bowl of food; she had hidden back there
for five days.
She came out gladly to eat by the
garage door—she would venture no farther.
She allowed us to pet her thin body briefly,
 on that rich orange fur that stood on end when any noise
disturbed her.
Salvaged now from the space she had decided to
die in, she stretched her paws back out into life.

Sometimes it Happens

Sometimes it happens
in moments of complete
repose
watching two pigeons in a ritual
circle dance around one another
by the roof air conditioners.
Or the steam from a
coffee cup that
the strangeness of LIFE
seeps in in an instant
of overwhelm.
What was it that assembled
this moment
the short darkening of sunlight
or a light bulb soft
dimming to half its brilliance?
Let a surgery appear
like a chimera on a red horizon
and everything presents as it
would if you saw it through
green glass.
A masterwork of form
and your age astonishes
you in the warm wrinkle of your hands—
the gray sag of skin beneath the eyes
and maybe a regret that
enters with you in an early afternoon
movie theater.
The bloat that expands
an hour or two in a single day
reminds you that blessings
may bulge into vision
early enough to encourage revision.
So LIFE prospers under the canopy

of confusion.
Remain content and happy with
a new image
like the insistent flutter of water birds
in the overbite of your remaining days.

Year's Flow

Waking up is a process.
~Brother David Steindl-Rast

Year's end has its own
aromas
the last few days scented
with stubborn memories
They begin on 28 December
and carry through the fireworks
at midnight
where odors of the year congeal
to celebrate their requiem
in unison.
I'm always asleep until
just before midnight
I rise to smell the Sulphur
in the sky that consumes all smells
but themselves.

Story Lines

This is the story/of a beautiful/lie
~Jorie Graham, "Reading Plato"

Appear everywhere.
    Where does the violent plot
of your life cut itself in two?
    Or in scraps to spread
its bewildered parts
        throughout each room
shuddering on its own foundation?
    Plot lines run hidden underground
yet surface in the cracked ceiling plaster
        and along the walls of your bedroom
alarming sleep.
    Lines perturb like itches
or fresh stitches uniting skin
        healing its tattered texture.
That's no child of mine.

What Opens You

To smell the March air of Spring,
the odor of the grape from the purple bushes
along Texas roads brings saliva seeping along
the sides of the tongue wanting to speak
in grape words.
Adorned by smell and their droopy smiles
is enough to melt me into myself
and out to the rows of grape-colored Bluebonnets
splashing everywhere now
with Indian Paint Brushes.
The earth loves to share her
colored past and present to anyone
who opens up along the roads
to greet the God who made you.
Then linger.
All internal clatter finds its right order.
What whistles through me is impermanence.

Words Awaken Memories

At times with closed gentleness
    and when called to with a power
that only gardens exhale in a breath
    of a red or purple bloom
Leopold digs next to where a squirrel
    covered a cache of nuts for a new year

Now more often I remember the past
    in clusters—bouquets really—of syllables
laid out in iambic rhythms to forge present's presence
    only living in silent air
can band words of affection in an arrangement
    that each life bequeaths to the next
small pair of hands that grab and squeeze
    the front of my shirt and scratch at
its row of buttons.

Specimen Temporarily Removed for Study

Lingering above the glass case
Held in place by the wood of an ancient
Pine tree.
I note droppings in the space
Now absent its treasure.

Alive, organic, restless in frieze
Unspoken sounds from the curtained
Entry to the back of the dusty museum.
I cannot imagine what alighted here
From a jungle-thick canopy of
Southern Peru:

"Only One Of Its Kind"
The yellowed index card insists that I believe,
With an apostrophe between "t"
And "s" later corrected by a
Tedious and hasty pencil.

"The Intuitive Slug Worm"
Is the species from the Genus
Pithy-can-tro-mon.
Yes! I can see it now.

What Was Today's Substitute?

Note the familiar; something is missing
a piece no longer there but the gap is filled
yet sometimes it is hard to put one's finger
on what is absent
forgiven perhaps as restitution
for yet another substitution
Can one live through days weeks
a life and not sense how the terms have changed
where a pale substitute lives in the space
vacated by a jewel so valuable
it went unnoticed and a small block
of something smelling unpleasant
stands in for the gem I treasured
then forgot until the odor
intruded as a meager replacement for loss
The new space is filled so why does it feel
So empty?
Remembering always yearns to replace
Forgetting
Lately the battle is a toss-up.

A Recent Death

Only the dead can grant us legitimacy.
~Robert Pogue Harrison, *The Dominion of the Dead*

In dreams I hear the voices of people
I have never met, the shades of earlier times
No telling from how deep in history they have pushed
Themselves out to address me in deep night
Their presence already opens my
Future in ways no planning could riff on
To be open receptive receiving echoes from
Where these voices dwell still ready
To speak something
But stopped perhaps by disease
A sudden death

Like my friend Marsha who collected
And studied mannequins
Enough to populate a small town
She knew their histories everyone
Now dead from cancer
I spoke to her two Thursdays ago
When she fretted about their fates
Before she died so suddenly

She now speaks to me in full presence
A sweet voice so soft and even
But with a laugh that had its own
Shape and format
Growing weaker on the phone
So faint now that I must wake to hear her
Truly.

Connection with Cosmos

One star blinks at me
from the dark sky outside
my study window before the day
became conscious of itself
it is all the light I need to read
to read the lines of my favorite poet
gleaning the star on the page
seeking the sun its source and present
deepened by starlight
the poet's words carry a tidy
galaxy of emotions right into
the room where each morning
early I search for its source
its serene whiteness to place
in my lap for tomorrow.

Turnstile Life

This is the heat that seeks the flaw in everything
And leaves the flaw.
~Jorie Graham, "Tennessee June"

Where were you when as-if on cue
the everyday arrived on time—slowed
to a stop
waited for you
who thought that something else
was more pressing than the present
so you delayed and the everyday
 tired of waiting for its turn in
your turnstile life
chugged out of the station
leaving you there alone, stationary
on the platform now deserted
wondering where the last 11 years had gone.
And their whenness; you wanted to be there
but past and future wiggled you loose
from ordinary presence.
Those days the ones unlived you can't compel
to return.
Remember the bursting bright fat yellow flower
balanced on top of a prickly pear cactus
along the road you walked yesterday?
For a moment a bee wondering what sweetness
lay within landed and descended into
the morning sun's beauty;
energized it flew off in dizzy ecstasy
buzzing Ss in the calm air.
But your thoughts blinded you to
this moment of everyday.
Now you can wait to catch the next train
To the final station marked "Done."

What We Might Have Done

If the weather had not turned so hot
the humidity a fluorescent lamp on
our forehead
or if we had learned to rise an hour earlier
or set the clock differently to a time we enjoy.

Remember the morning the truck refused to start?
It was the day for heroic action
instead I watched talk shows and
the weather channel waiting for
hours for the Triple A mechanic
to jump-start the battery
or that itch to buy lottery tickets
because the date was 7/17/17?

Nothing clicked on those days
something missing.
I need a more current fiction
To sustain me.

When As-If

     Nothing knows the future
Better than the past.
     History is the time of sure ground
Beneath bare feet.
     The present is undecided
The future reluctant to commit.
     To shift from what-is
To what if
     Or from what is not
To as-if frees my bordered mirror
     To reflect back to me what is not yet.

And yet the images appear as-if
     They were truer than
The sketched life whose
     Focus has always leaned toward
What if.

     A poem smells the scents
of not yet but maybe so.
     I can live with that.
A poem takes things that
     Act as-if they were true.
Noticing is optional
     Belief necessary.

Sometimes

Oh how we want/to be taken/and changed
~Jorie Graham, "Scirocco"

I take a new road
perhaps not far
new is better than far
an old habit interrupted
a quick reaction withheld
a familiar resentment
stopped at the light
Let it idle there.

Sometimes a moment of peace
descends from somewhere
I've not traveled to in a long time

Sometimes I sleep in
just for the fun of trespassing
on a smug routine
and sometimes I do in midweek
what I used to allow only on weekends
or payday.

Yes, sometimes I feel
a grateful sense of freedom
from all wants cares and confusions
I've named it a sometime moment
of sacred serene

And sometimes I am urged to look back
over a range of seven decades and
glimpse not one regret

Sometimes all is as it should be
Absent all typos, fragments or white-outs
Perhaps sometimes is all the time we have

When compassion slips through
the cracks of our imperfections
Sometimes it cannot be otherwise

Arrangement

This morning in darkness
things begin to present themselves
in a way I cannot know them
a slanted moment because
I discover the unknowable underside
of what I had forgotten in the
silk folds of time passing beneath my feet
now a strange life ruffles
the curtains of a new space
 to recollect all the small shards
of colored glass
that dare me to set them next to
one another in right order
to form the shape of my past
so I can wake tomorrow
and know my time has meant more
than I planned on
more than I wished for
more than I deserved

Story

Your story is the thing
        inside you
   Folding always in
             on itself
Plotting its own future
         out of a foregone
           past.
In the central casting room
       of your story
  A secret reveals itself
          in layers
Only to itself   before dawn
       before you wake.
  Its time is brief
before change overtakes it
   To form a new tale
One that tells   one that tolls
     under the pressure of
  that unlived part of itself
Swelling
    in the same room—

Acknowledgments

"Sutures" in Voice Magazine, Santa Barbara, California. 21 July 2017, p. 20.

"Night Life" in Voice Magazine, Friday, December 8, 2017, Santa Barbara, California, p. 20.

POET BIOGRAPHIES

Craig Deininger earned an MFA in Poetry from the University of Massachusetts at Amherst and a PhD in Mythological Studies from Pacifica Graduate Institute in California. He makes his living as a construction worker in Iowa, California, and in Colorado where he teaches Jungian Psychology at Naropa University. He also teaches myth and archetype to storytellers and film-students at Studio School in Los Angeles. Presently, he is working to establish an industrial hemp company in California in support of the urgent need to reverse worldwide environmental damages incurred by unsustainable practices, outdated legislation, and a long list of unconscionable financial, political, and industrial institutions.

Dennis Patrick Slattery, PhD, is emeritus faculty in the Mythological Studies Program at Pacifica Graduate Institute in California. He has authored, co-authored, edited or co-edited 26 volumes and has published over 200 articles in books, journals, magazines, newspapers and on-line journals. This is his 7th. volume of poetry. He offers talks and riting retreats in the United States, Canada, Ireland and Europe as well as webinars on discovering one's personal myth and related subjects. He is currently finishing a book on Homer's *Odyssey* as well as a co-authored work, *Deep Creativity: 7 Ways to Spark Your Artistic Spirit* with Jennifer Leigh Selig and Deborah Anne Quibell. For the past 6 years he has been taking classes in acrylic and watercolor painting and has produced 20 works.

www.dennispslattery.com and dslattery@pacifica.edu.